In Every Blade
of Rustling Grass

STOLEN FROM THE LIBRARY
OF

Dr. Paul E. Sago

In Every Blade *of* Rustling Grass

Meditations on Looking
and Listening for God

Bass M. Mitchell

DIMENSIONS
FOR LIVING
NASHVILLE

IN EVERY BLADE OF RUSTLING GRASS:
MEDITATIONS ON LOOKING AND LISTENING FOR GOD

By Bass M. Mitchell

Copyright © 2000 by Dimensions for Living

Library of Congress Cataloging-in-Publication Data

Mitchell, Bass M., 1955-
    In every blade of rustling grass : meditations on looking and listening / Bass M. Mitchell.
        p. cm.
    ISBN 0-687-08429-6 (alk. paper)
    1. Christian life—Meditations.   2. Mitchell, Bass M., 1955-   I. Title.

BV4501.2 .M538 2000
242—dc21

99-058457

This book is printed on acid-free paper.

00 01 02 03 04 05 06 07 08 09—10 9 8 7 6 5 4 3 2 1

MANUFACTURED IN THE UNITED STATES OF AMERICA

I dedicate this book

to my wife, Debbie,

and our children,

Michael and Meredith.

Through these three

special gifts,

God has taught me so much.

Contents

Introduction

𝒜 MINISTER ONCE TOLD HIS CONGREGATION, "THERE is a sermon in every blade of grass." Later that week the minister was out mowing his lawn when a church member drove by, stopped, and shouted, "That's right, Preacher. Cut those sermons short!"

One of the most significant things I have learned as a Christian is that there really is a sermon in every blade of grass. Every day, every moment, in countless ways God comes to us, seeks to speak to us. God is not just out there somewhere—transcendent, distant, the Holy Other. God is also here—immanent. God is around us. God is in us. In Acts we read, "So that they would search for God and perhaps grope for him and find him—though indeed he is not far from each one of us. For 'In him we live and move and have our being' " (Acts 17:27-28).

Yet we tend to compartmentalize our religious lives, divide them into sacred times and places. Sunday for many is that time we give some attention to the divine in our lives. What this time really should do is help us know that God is related to every part of our lives every day. Then we would begin to discover that all times, all places, are sacred and holy, filled with the presence and voice of God. All ground is holy ground.

The Incarnation teaches us this. God chose to come to us in flesh and blood, in a child born to a peasant man and woman. God comes to us in the ordinary. This is one of the most wonderful things Jesus taught us— to look for God in the ordinary. Just read the teachings of Jesus and see how he saw and heard God every-where—in a coin, a fish net, a lamp, fruit trees, chil-dren, salt, a cup, a loaf of bread. In all things he found some lesson God would teach us. Jesus taught us that the fingerprints of God are all around us, if we have eyes to see. The voice of God constantly fills the air, if we have ears to hear.

Maltbie Babcock knew this well and expressed it in one of my favorite hymns:

> *This is my Father's world,*
> *the birds their carols raise,*
> *the morning light,*
> *the lily white,*
> *declare their maker's praise.*
>
> *This is my Father's world:*
> *he shines in all that's fair;*
> *in the rustling grass*
> *I hear him pass,*
> *he speaks to me everywhere.*

At this very moment each one of us is being bombarded literally with thousands of sound waves of all kinds. We do not know it or recognize it until we turn on a radio in our car or home. Then a whole new world of sound, music, news is opened to us. It is there all along but not until we turn on the radio and listen.

The voice of God, like radio waves, surrounds us, permeates our world, too. Each of us has a radio, a kind of spiritual receiver inside us that we can use to pick up those messages, that enables us to hear God. It's a kind of sixth sense. We have five senses: taste, smell, sight, hearing, touch. This sixth sense uses all these other senses in seeking to open us to the presence of God that is as close to us as our breath.

I love learning about Native Americans. One of the most fascinating things is how they can follow the trail of animals and find their way through the wilderness by reading signs. They can see things all around them that I am sure I probably would not because I do not know how to look. They do.

This sixth sense is the one we develop to help us look for God signs, those events, great and small, in our daily lives that reveal the presence of God. This means being able to read the world spiritually, listening to hear God, expecting to catch God doing something in our lives and in our world. Thus we are constantly wide-eyed with anticipation.

The problem is that this sixth sense is often under-used, stunted. We need this sixth sense honed, sharpened, developed. We need to learn how to turn on this inner radio, how to adjust our spiritual antenna so that we begin to hear the ever-present voice of God.

I like to walk on the trails that wind their way through the ancient mountains around our home. I look forward to it. But sometimes I am almost at the top of the mountain before I realize where I am. It's like I put myself on autopilot or "autowalk" in this case. My body is there, surrounded by the trees, the wonder of God's creation everywhere; but my mind is distracted, filled with what I have to do when I get back home. I have to force myself to listen, to be present where I am. Then slowly the distractions begin to fade, and I begin to truly be where I am. I begin to hear God pass in the rustling grass.

One of the keys to hearing and experiencing God in our daily lives is to be fully present in all we do. We need to give our whole selves to whatever duties or responsibilities each moment brings, knowing that in them and through them God is also present, God is speaking. It is being attentive to the present, not obsessed with the past or the future, not driven from one distraction to another. Sometimes the present brings a moment to sit quietly at the feet of Jesus (like Mary), and other moments find us on our knees scrubbing the kitchen floor (like Martha). One moment we are on a walk in the forest, another we are at a desk piled high with work. Whatever the present brings, God is there, God is speaking, if we give ourselves to each moment, if we look and listen with that sixth sense that enables us to find that one needful thing Jesus spoke of to Mary—that wondrous sense of the presence of the Divine.

This book is a collection of my own God sightings throughout my life—from childhood to the present—and some reflection on what I feel God was teaching me through them. You will notice that I find God in not just one type of experience but in the everyday ups and downs of life. God is in the joy and the sorrow. God is in life and in death. God's voice can be heard in times of laughter and in times of weeping.

Each of these reflections cites a reading from the Bible. A knowledge of the Bible greatly assists me in seeing God signs all around me. In a way the Bible is also a collection of God sightings, of how God's people over the centuries have seen God at work in their lives. By making those stories and teachings a part of us, our spiritual vision and hearing are enhanced; for that same God is as present for us as for them. Also, as we become more and more aware of God's presence in our lives, those experiences give us new insight into the teachings of the Bible, helping us to better understand and relate it to our lives and our world.

One final note. I offer these stories and reflections only as examples of just how and when and where we can hear God pass in our lives. My prayer is that they will assist you in becoming more present wherever you may be, so that you will not miss the God who speaks to us in every blade of rustling grass.

Magic Wands

The LORD said to [Moses], "What is that in your
hand?" He said, "A rod." And [God] said, "Cast
it on the ground." So he cast it on the ground,
and it became a serpent; and Moses fled from it.
(Exodus 4:2-3, RSV)

I MUST HAVE BEEN ABOUT TEN YEARS OLD THE FIRST
time I heard the story of Moses in Sunday school. It
has been one of my favorites. I remember thinking
how great it would be to float down the river in a
basket or to have a neat stick like Moses. So I took
an old potato basket out of the shed and called my
little brother, Danny, down to the river (we lived
only a couple of hundred feet from the Neuse River
in North Carolina). After some convincing on my
part, as well as a few promises to give him some of
my favorite baseball cards, I got him to get into the
basket and proceeded to try to float him down the
river. (I really wanted to be in the basket myself, but
just in case, well, you know. Anyway, what are
brothers for if not to use?) Well, that basket sank
like a brick. Danny got his new Sunday clothes wet
and ran sobbing and dripping to the house. I knew

that our mother would not be very happy, even if what I did was biblical.

Next I went out in the woods to cut my own magic stick. (I thought it was a good idea to go to the woods under the circumstances.) I picked out a stick that I thought must have looked a lot like the one Moses had. I spent the afternoon trying to do all kinds of tricks with it. But I could not turn the river red, except for some red clay from the bank that I rubbed on the end of the stick. To be truthful, I thought about trying to turn the stick into a snake; but I have always been scared of snakes.

All this came back to me as I was shaving one morning. My little girl, Meredith, about five years old then, came in to watch me. She finds shaving a most curious and funny activity. I have even seen her trying to twist and contort her face like I do. That morning she managed to climb up on the bathroom vanity and sat staring at me. I knew she was up to something, so I just let her sit there. She was holding a white stick with a small crystal ball on the end.

Finally, looking me over, she said, "Daddy, do you want me to use my magic wand to make you handsome?"

I stopped shaving and looked at her. "No, I'll just stay ugly," I said.

"Come on, Daddy. Let me make you handsome," she insisted.

"Okay. Make me handsome."

She made a few movements with the wand and mumbled something. Then she studied me for a moment and said, "Daddy, it didn't work. Can I try again?"

At that point I chased her little giggling body out of the bathroom.

Later she told me, "Daddy, I was just kidding. You are handsome," and she hugged my neck.

Don't you wish sometimes we had a real magic wand for the church? Moses had a staff that could turn into a snake, turn the Nile red, and even draw water from a rock. Wouldn't it be great to have a magic staff, one that we could wave in the air and Whoosh! Beautiful facilities appear. Whoosh! The offerings are tripled. Whoosh! The worship services are overflowing with people. Whoosh! Everything is exactly as we want it to be, so there is no need for anymore meetings. Whoosh! Everyone likes us and cannot say enough good things about us. They even think the way we do!

But life does not work that way. There are no magic wands for us. When you think about it, God's greatest instrument in this story from Exodus was not a piece of wood but a person—Moses. God chooses to work through human lives.

There are no shortcuts on the road of discipleship, no magic tricks. If we are to do what God has called us to do, it will take time, commitment, giving, faith, self-sacrifice, love, patience—all the things that Moses had to give.

Lord, help us give ourselves this and every day to you as your wands in the world, the instruments through which you can do wondrous things for the good of your Kingdom. Amen.

I Love Ladders

Hold me up, that I may be safe
and have regard for your
statutes continually.
(Psalm 119:117)

MY FATHER WAS A CARPENTER. OFTEN MY BROTHER and I would spend the summer helping him build houses. One of my jobs was to do most of the painting. I'll never forget the summer when I was standing on top of an old wooden ladder painting the gable end of a house. I felt the ladder shift under me and realized just in time that it was going to topple over. Somehow I managed to grab the edge of the roof just as the ladder fell. There I was—hanging onto the roof with one hand, a paint brush in the other. In addition, I do not know how it happened, but somehow the handle on the paint bucket got attached to my shoe. If only I could have gotten this on videotape!

I yelled for help. My brother came running around the side of the house. He stopped and looked up at me and started laughing. (I should have never put him in that basket and tried to float him down the river like

Moses or all the other stuff I did to him. There was an evil gleam in his eye.)

"What you doing up there?" he finally asked with a smirk.

"Just hanging around," I said. "Now put that ladder back up!"

"No can do," he said; and the smile had left his face. He was looking at the ladder. I looked at it too and saw that it was broken. I was about to tell my brother to come under me (so I could fall on him—just kidding) when I noticed he had left. (Guess he had learned a few things since the basket and the river.)

In what seemed like an eternity, he came running back around the corner. "Dad's gone down the street for another ladder. There's a construction crew down there," he yelled up at me.

At that point I let go of the paint brush and held onto the edge of the roof with both hands. My arms felt like they were going to break. I did not think I could make it or that my father would get back in time.

My brother kept saying, "Don't let go. Hang on. The ladder's coming. Dad's bringing the ladder."

And he did. The most beautiful sight I have ever seen was that aluminum ladder. To this day the sight of a ladder gives me a warm fuzzy feeling.

Lots of times in my life as a Christian I have been in a similar situation. Everything under me has seemed to fall away, and all I have to cling to is my faith. But all the while there are those shouting words of encouragement, "Don't let go. Don't give up. The ladder's on the way."

One cold winter when my son was but an infant, I was unemployed. We did not even have enough money to buy fuel for heat. The pipes froze inside the house. Things were about as bleak as I have ever faced. And then, when I thought I could not hold on any longer, a letter arrived in the mail with a job offer. What a wondrous ladder!

Lord, we get so weary sometimes. Our arms ache. Our hearts break. Our spirits deflate. We just do not know how much longer we can hold on. Thanks for the encouragers you send who will not let us let go. Thanks too for the ladders we know are on their way. Even if they do not get here in time, Lord, if our strength fails us, we still are going to trust you; for you are our strength, our ladder. Amen.

A B-O-M-B in Gilead

Is there no balm in Gilead?
Is there no physician there?
Why then has the health of my
poor people
not been restored?
(Jeremiah 8:22)

GOING TO CHURCH SERVICES CAN BE A STRANGE AND confusing experience for children (for adults too). We make the mistake of assuming everyone understands what is happening. But the things we do and the kind of language we use do not always translate for children, so they put these unknowns into words and images they can understand.

It was Christmas and the minister read the Christmas story—about the angels, shepherds, and the baby Jesus. When one little girl got home, she said to her mother, "I really like that story about the shepherds; but tell me, Mom, why were the shepherds out washing their socks by night?"

Another little boy was called up in front of the congregation by his Sunday school teacher to recite the Twenty-third Psalm. Obviously he must have often gone fishing with his father; for when he got to the fourth verse, he said, "Thy rod and thy reel, they comfort me."

Even the Lord's Prayer, which we use all the time and think everyone understands, can confuse children.

A little fellow prayed, "Our Father who art in heaven, Harold be thy name." And then, "Give us this day our daily bread, and liberty and justice for all."

What really confused me in church as a child were the hymns. Three stand out in my memory.

One of them was stanza 2 of "Come, Thou Fount of Every Blessing." It begins, "Here I raise mine Ebenezer. . . ." I had no idea what this meant. Was the hymn writer the mother of Ebenezer Scrooge? Was an Ebenezer some pet you raised? If so, I wanted one.

Another hymn that puzzled me was "Bringing in the Sheaves." I would not have known a sheaf if I sat on one. I thought for a while that we were singing, "Bringing in the Sheets." That made a whole lot more sense to me because I had helped my mother do that.

The hymn we sang that confused me the most was the "Bomb Song," as I called it: "There Is a Bomb in Gilead." I had no idea where Gilead was, yet I wondered why no one seemed all that concerned about it. I mean, shouldn't we have called the bomb squad or something?

Fortunately, I had someone I could talk with about these concerns—Mrs. Pate, my first Sunday school teacher. She told us every Sunday, "If you ever have a question, please know that you can always come to me about it." I believed her. So I took my questions about these strange hymns to her. She patiently explained that Ebenezer was what a man named Samuel called a stone. He wanted his people to think about how God had helped them when they saw that stone.

"Sheaves?" Well, that's an image often used in the Bible and one that farmers have been familiar with for centuries. It refers to stalks of grain like wheat or barley that are cut down and then tied into bundles and sometimes stacked leaning against one another in the fields. Bringing those sheaves to the barn was the harvest time, a time of great joy and celebration. Bringing them in is a way of talking about bringing people to Christ, she explained.

Mrs. Pate told me that it was not a bomb in Gilead but a "balm," a medicine that people in the days of Jeremiah received in a village called "Gilead." "Where do we go when we are sick?" she asked. I told her, "The doctor." "Yes, and the doctor gives us what?" "Medicine," I replied. Then she tried to explain how Jesus was kind-of like a balm or medicine God gives to help us feel better. Well, everything made more sense; but I still did not understand fully what she was saying.

I learned from this experience, however, that there is always someone I can go to when I have questions (and I still do). I also learned that Sunday school is not the only place we can learn. Worship each Sunday is filled with teachable moments, for we must not assume that everyone understands even the words of a hymn we sing. So I often tell the children who attend, "If you have a question about anything, you can always ask me." And I find myself surveying their faces (and the faces of the adults) while we sing hymns or anything else for signs that someone hears a bomb ticking in Gilead.

Teaching God, you created us with a strong sense of curiosity, of asking questions and seeking answers. Each day is a day of learning, a day at your school; and your whole world is a classroom where you teach us wondrous things. We thank and praise you for the other teachers you give us to whom we can always go with our questions, who never see any questions as "dumb" but who patiently seek to instruct us in your wisdom. Most of all, thank you for Jesus, the Master Teacher, whose words are like a healing balm for our souls. Amen.

The Story Game

Then our mouth was FILLED WITH LAUGHTER,
and our tongue with SHOUTS OF JOY.
(Psalm 126:2a, capitals added)

A MERRY HEART doeth good like a medicine:
but a broken spirit drieth the bones.
(Proverbs 17:22 in KJV, capitals added)

*G*OD GIVES US HUMOR TO HELP US COPE WITH LIFE. Laughter is like a shock absorber on a car. It helps us absorb the bumps and get over the potholes. Laughter can sometimes keep us moving along when the road gets steep and the going gets tough.

We were driving to North Carolina recently, a six-hour trip, to visit our relatives. One of the great problems families face is how to get any place in a car together without hating or strangling one another. To help us survive our trips, we often sing songs and play games. This time we started playing "The Story Game," which works like this: One person begins a story and then stops, turning it over to the next person to continue. The story goes around to everyone until it comes to an end. As you can imagine, this process results in some, how shall I say it, interesting stories.

I started the story that day: "Once upon a time there was a little girl. Her father made a swing for her from rope and wood and hung it from the limb of a large tree. As the girl was swinging, she heard something behind her. She turned and looked and there was. . . ." Then I turned the story over to Debbie, my wife. Debbie added to the story and then turned it over to Michael. Somehow Michael turned the little girl into Indiana Jones. "Indiana Jones went in this cave," Michael said. "And he saw a chest, and he opened it, and . . . You take it, Meredith," he said.

Meredith (who was about six years old at the time) was not ready to take it; but she knew she had to say something, so she said, "And then he went outside and went for a walk in his car. . . ."

We all turned and looked at her and said, "Huh?"

She burst out all over in giggles. When Meredith starts giggling, she can hardly stop. So, we joined her.

We must have laughed for thirty minutes. I saw a car pass us with a family in it. They were staring at us like they were wondering what we had been drinking or if perhaps we had been on the road a little too long and the same fate might await them. (I did see them turn off at the next rest stop.)

I often wondered what I would have done if a state highway patrolman had pulled me over about then. He would have asked me to get out of the car to explain; and all I would have been able to say was, "He went for a walk in his car." After which the patrolman would have had me taking a walk to his car.

We continued to play the story game the rest of that

trip, and at some point in every story one of us would have to have the character "go for a walk in his car." Then we would burst out laughing again. It certainly made that trip easier.

Laughter is God's way of helping make life's journey easier.

I think the world needs much from the church. But one of the most powerful witnesses we give is the sound of our laughter as the family journeys together. Maybe others will want to join us and find out what is so much fun.

God, if it is true that we are made in your image, then you must enjoy laughter. We thank you for this great and good gift that often breaks tension, that gives a lift when we are feeling low, that brings added joy to the journey—a gift we can give to a world that very much needs it. Amen.

Christianity
in the Car

People with a hot temper do foolish things;
wiser people remain calm.
(Proverbs 14:17, TEV)

I WAS DRIVING HOME FROM CHARLOTTESVILLE, VIRGINIA. Everything was going fine until I got to Staunton. I stopped at the first stoplight. Something on the seat had fallen to the floor, so I reached down to pick it up. While I did, the light turned green. A car horn blasted. I glanced in the rear-view mirror and saw an angry face in the car behind me. I started through the intersection, only to have this driver whip out and zoom past, shouting at me and making some, how shall I say, creative hand gestures. All this because I spent two seconds too long at a green light!

After that, every stoplight in Staunton caught me. I began to believe it was a plot, that someone somewhere changed them just as I approached.

When I was finally a couple of miles outside the city, I rounded a corner; and there was the largest skunk I have ever seen. It was trying to cross the road. It did not make it. I did not think I was going to make it either.

Apparently I am allergic to the smell of skunk because I started sneezing. When I start sneezing, it lasts awhile.

Did you ever sneeze while you were driving? Do you know how difficult it is to keep your eyes open when you sneeze? So there I was with one hand on the steering wheel, one pinching my nose, and my head out the window.

Soon after the skunk incident, a car pulled out ahead of me. I had to put on the brakes to keep from running into it. It sped along at the incredible rate of thirty-five miles per hour! There was no place I could pass. Finally, this snail crawled off the road. No sooner had he left, than another slow-moving car pulled in front of me. It was a plot, I tell you! A conspiracy!

No sooner had the second slowpoke pulled off than I looked in my rear-view mirror and saw the blazing headlights of an eighteen-wheeler barreling toward me. There was no place for him to pass or no area for me to pull over. He just got closer and closer, his headlights still glaring in my eyes. I finally found a place to pull over, sliding on the gravel as I did so; and he roared past. I looked both ways. Nothing coming, so I pulled back onto the road. Thirty seconds later another truck was on my bumper. It was a plot! I could almost hear the truckers on their CB's, "Breaker one nine. The Reverend just pulled over. Passed him. I see him pulling back onto the road. You can come on up now. Your turn. Ten four." Before I got home that night, I had to pull over five times.

A lifetime of driving experience came together that night for me in this profound insight: If you can be a Christian in your car, you can be a Christian anywhere. I do not know about you, but every time I get in the car my Christianity is tested. Sometimes I pass, and sometimes I fail.

That night, when I finally got home, I was angry. I wanted to go back and find that man in Staunton who started the whole nightmare and throw the dead skunk into his car. The degree of my road rage surprised and frightened me. So I decided to do a little Bible study on anger. I was surprised at how many of the wise sayings in Proverbs have to do with anger.

"If you cannot control your anger, you are as helpless as a city without walls, open to attack" (25:28, TEV).

"Hot tempers cause arguments, but patience brings peace" (15:18, TEV).

"It is better to be patient than powerful. It is better to win control over yourself than over whole cities" (16:32, TEV).

"If you are sensible, you will control your temper. When someone wrongs you, it is a great virtue to ignore it" (19:11, TEV).

"Stupid people express their anger openly, but sensible people are patient and hold it back" (29:11, TEV).

"A gentle answer quiets anger, but a harsh one stirs it up" (15:1, TEV).

James 1:19 gives the wise advice to be quick to listen and slow to speak, and you will be slow to become angry.

Jesus also taught about anger. The Old Testament law declares, he said, that anyone who commits murder will be judged; but "now I tell you: whoever is angry with his brother will be brought to trial" (Matthew 5:22, TEV). Have a heart so full of love that there is never any room for even an angry feeling toward your brother or sister.

Lots of good advice here. I did not feel so angry after reading the verses. But, of course, Jesus and the wise teachers in Proverbs never drove a car, did they?

Lord, sometimes our emotions get the best of us. Sometimes they scare us. Sometimes we seem at their mercy. Give us the mind and spirit of Christ who was able to use even his emotions in your service. Amen.

Forget It

I will forgive their iniquity, and remember their sin no more. (Jeremiah 31:34b)

*G*OT A MINUTE? I HAVE TO SHARE THIS WITH SOMEONE. It was embarrassing. There I was sitting in my office at 12:30 P.M. The phone rang. On the other end of the line I heard the worried and slightly agitated voice of a woman. She said, "Are you OK? Where are you? You were supposed to pick me up forty minutes ago. Has your watch stopped? Can you tell time? Didn't you get that far in school?"

As you may have guessed, the woman was my wife. I had forgotten to pick her up for lunch. She was not happy.

I was not too happy about it either, for a lot of reasons, not the least of which was that I would never ever be allowed to forget that I had forgotten.

I began to wonder if age was catching up with me. Someone once told me that there are three signs of old age. The first one is forgetfulness. I cannot remember the other two.

I believe it was the same fellow, cannot remember for sure, who asked me if I knew why God does not let older people have children. "Why is that?" I asked. "Cause they'd lay them down somewhere and forget where they put them!"

Maybe my memory loss is because I have moved closer to Washington, DC. Maybe it is something in the water or air there that's seeping down here. Seems that a lot of our officials are suffering from memory loss. The standard reply when being grilled by a congressional committee is, "I don't recall, Senator," or "Not to my recollection." Is it wise to put persons in control of things who have such poor memories?

Forgetfulness plays big in Hollywood too. One of the most popular movies in recent years is about forgetfulness. A family is caught up in the hecticness of Christmas, trying to get to the airport to fly to Paris. Halfway across the ocean the mother shouts, "Kevin!" Seems that little Kevin, her youngest son, was left *Home Alone*.

I suppose forgetfulness is not all bad. Depends on what or whom you forget. There are certainly things we need to remember so that we do not let them happen again. It also seems to me, however, that a lot of things in our lives, especially from the past, need to be forgotten. I have a feeling that much pain of body and mind can be traced to an inability or unwillingness to forget.

Maybe nations, too, would be better off if they did

not have such good memories. Just imagine. Suddenly, cases of memory loss break out and spread among the populations of Northern Ireland or South Africa or the Middle East or America. Forgotten are the injustices, the hatred and bitterness of the past, the racism. . . . All that is left are people, human beings with another chance to make better memories together. Maybe a good dose of amnesia would be just the thing to help make the world a better place.

I'm glad to hear God saying through the prophet Isaiah, "I, I am He / who blots out your transgressions for my own sake, / and I will not remember your sins" (Isaiah 43:25) or through the psalmist that God "does not deal with us according to our sins, nor repay us according to our iniquities. . . . [A]s far as the east is from the west, so far [God] removes our transgressions from us (Psalm 103:10, 12). God chooses to forgive and utterly forget. I could stand to be more like that.

Excuse me a moment. My phone's ringing.

"Hello? Yes, dear. I won't forget. 11:50. That's A.M., not P.M. Got it. No, I won't forget. Yes, I know where to go. Yes, that's exactly one hour, fifteen minutes, and twenty-five seconds from now. Right. Yes, my watch is correct. No, it's still running. No, no need to call me again. Yes, I'll remember. . . ."

Sorry that took so long. What were we talking about? I forget.

Lord, we are grateful that you often choose to have a poor memory, forgiving and forgetting our sins, casting them from your mind to the depths of the ocean and the height of the sky. Help us to be more like you, forgetting those things we do not need to remember but remembering always your blessings. Amen.

Jesus Visits the K & W

Now all the tax collectors and sinners were coming near to listen to him [Jesus, that is]. And the Pharisees and the scribes were grumbling and saying, *"This fellow welcomes sinners and eats with them."* (Luke 15:1-2, italics added)

O NE OF MY FAVORITE PLACES TO EAT IS K & W CAFETE-RIA. I usually eat there on Monday, my day off, and every other opportunity I get.

A few Mondays ago I drove to Roanoke, Virginia. At a couple of stoplights near the mall, there were those people, you have seen them, standing in the median holding a sign that says, "Hungry. Unemployed. Will work for food." Well, I, like everyone else, just ignored them. They looked rough, and I imagined they smelled even worse. Besides, they were probably crooks or winos. After all, it was my day off.

I pulled into the K & W parking lot, picked up the morning paper from the car seat, strolled inside, stood in line, and got the delicious veggies that I craved.

I had hardly sat down and opened the paper when I noticed some murmuring and heads turning. In the line were a couple of those men I had seen standing out on the road. There was another man with them, obviously not one of them but one of us—the normal, clean, employed people. He had picked these men up, brought them there, and was buying them a meal.

Everyone in the cafeteria watched them. I thought that maybe he would just buy them the meal and then he would leave, inflicting them on us normal, employed, clean folks. No. He bought himself a meal, walked over to the booth beside me with them, and sat down. Then he talked to them, and I heard them laugh a few times together. The man even went back through the line and got them desserts. I left before they did.

How rude of that man to interrupt my time, my day off. God, do not do that to me anymore on my day off. Do not send Jesus to the K & W on Monday. Try Tuesday. There is a special that day. If you persist, I will have to go to McDonald's next time. I know. He goes there too. Maybe I just will not take any more days off.

God, you are always on duty. I thank you that you never take time off, that you never slumber or sleep, that there is not a day, hour, or moment that you withhold from me your presence and compassion. Help me see the needy around me through your eyes. Help me see them not as interruptions but as opportunities to share your love. Amen.

No Deposit, No Return

Train children in the right way,
and when old, they will not
stray. (Proverbs 22:6)

Bring [up your children] in the discipline and
instruction of the Lord. (Ephesians 6:4)

*T*HIS WEEK I DID SOMETHING THAT I HAVE WANTED TO do for a long time. I opened two saving accounts in the local bank—one for my son and the other for my daughter. I looked in my wallet and realized that I did not have very much to deposit. But it was a start, and I plan to add to the accounts as often as I can. Over time and with some interest, perhaps the accounts will amount to something of value. You see, I want the accounts to be something that my son and daughter can draw on in the future whenever they have need of them. When they need the money, it will be there.

As I walked out of the bank, God did it to me again! I wish God would stop sneaking up on me! Yes, God spoke to me. All I was trying to do was get to the bank and back home, but God met me in the bank parking lot. God just loves interrupting my day. God is a teacher who thinks every place is a classroom and every moment is a teachable one.

Well, what was the lesson for the day? I sat there in my car, gripping the steering wheel, looking at the bank; and a voice came to me saying, "Good thing you did today, Bass. You love your children, depositing your hard-earned money there for them. But what are you depositing in their hearts? What wealth are you storing in their minds that they might draw on when they need it in the days and years ahead of them?"

"Uh, I'm not sure I understand. . . ."

The voice came back, "What treasure of values, of ethics, of love for God and neighbor are you building up in them? No deposit, no return, you know."

Lord, I am reminded this day that my children are really your children, that you have just entrusted them to me for this time. May I love them and teach them as you would. May they see in me a love for and a closeness to you that they would want for themselves. For, after all, Lord, I know that of all I can give them, nothing is more important than to lead them to know and love you. Amen.

And a Little Child Shall Lead Them

Then he took a child and put it among them. . . .
(Mark 9:36)

"Truly I tell you, whoever does not receive the
kingdom of God as a little child will never enter
it." And he took them up in his arms, laid his
hands on them, and blessed them. (Mark 10:15-
16, italics added)

*A*S I REFLECTED ON THE LECTIONS FOR THE FOLLOWING
Sunday, all dealing in some manner with money matters, I thought back to a children's message I gave
years ago.

I showed the children the offering plates and asked
them to tell me what the plates were for. They all knew
that we put money in them.

Then I asked them if they knew why we did this.
They looked kind of confused (as did some of the people in the congregation, confused and a little concerned
at the direction this conversation was taking).

I explained that we give money for lots of reasons
but mainly to say "Thank you!" to God for all the
blessings God gives us. Giving our money helps
remind us that all we have comes from God, that we
are dependent on God for everything. It is a way of
helping the church spread the news all over the world

that God loves us all and of helping the church feed people and care for people in many ways.

Then I gave each child ten pennies. I explained the tithe, that is, that it would be one penny from the ten. And I told them about making an offering, which to me means that which we give beyond the tithe, that is, two pennies or more.

Then I asked the children to put their tithes and offerings in the plates before they went out to children's worship.

A couple turned and ran out, clutching their pennies in tight little fists . . . (to the nervous laughter of some in the congregation).

Others came forward (somewhat gloomily) and dropped a penny in the plate . . . (to the silence of the congregation).

Others dropped in a penny and one or two other pennies . . . (some smiled in the congregation).

The last child, a bright faced little girl with long brown hair tied with a yellow ribbon, went to the table, stepped up on a step before it since she was so short, and looked wide-eyed with wonder into the plate. She slowly put her hands over the plate, since it took both hands to hold the pennies, and let them all fall into the plate, the sound echoing through the sanctuary. Then she turned and bounded out of the door in joy while some of the congregation looked kind of uneasy and others joyous.

Moved myself, I turned to the congregation and could only say, "I do not think I need to preach today."

Loving God, Jesus came and taught us so many things and through such unexpected means. He taught us about simple faith and trust through holding up the most powerless among us still—children. May I not be childish but childlike in my trust, in my giving, in my love this and every day. Make me ever aware and alert to the many ways you teach us through others, especially the little ones you still hold and bless in your arms. Amen.

Mirror Lakes

We all reflect as in a mirror the splendour of
the Lord; thus we are transfigured into his like-
ness, from splendour to splendour; such is the
influence of the Lord who is Spirit.
(2 Corinthians 3:18, NEB)

*O*N A FAMILY VACATION WE HAPPENED BY LURAY, Virginia, and went into the famous Luray Caverns. Soon we found ourselves in a strange, new world. The cool, misty air filled our lungs, a welcome change from the humidity and heat in the outside world. The whole place was like God's sculpturing studio. Minute-to-massive rock figures in multicolors rose majestically from the ground and hung from the ceiling. Occasionally a drop of sediment-rich water would drip on our faces as we looked up, reminding us that the infinitely patient and ceaseless process that created all of this was still at work.

But of all we saw that day the most interesting and inspiring to me was "Mirror Lake." It is a section of the caverns that is covered with about eight to ten inches of water. The water is practically invisible. Had the guide not told us it was there, we would have been completely unaware of it. Such was the perfection of its reflective power. I reached out and touched the water just to see if it was really there.

As I stood there thinking about how this tiny lake reflects perfectly the beauty of the ceiling above it, it came to me that this is what I have been striving for in my Christian life—to be a mirror lake, to perfectly reflect the One above, whose love is so wondrous. I had to admit that often I am a poor reflector, a tiny, dingy lake. But somehow I felt renewed and encouraged. If that little lake can so flawlessly reflect the beauty of God's handiwork, then surely I, with the help of the Spirit, can reflect in my life the beauty of Christ.

Lord, help me to become a mirror so close to the Christ that he is perfectly reflected in me. Amen.

Bunting

If any want to become my followers, let them
deny themselves and take up their cross and
follow me. For those who want to save their
life, will lose it, and those who lose their life
for my sake, and for the sake of the gospel, will
save it. (Mark 8:34-35)

*W*E WERE PACKING TO MOVE TO THE BEAUTIFUL
mountains of Bath County, Virginia. My son, Michael,
came across a blue, dusty picture album. He looked
through it and came running to me. It was a collection
of pictures and news clippings from my youthful summer days spent on the baseball field. One picture of me
on a team caught my son's attention. I was about his age
when it was taken. He had no trouble picking me out,
but he did have some problem believing that I was once
his size and age.

That album, especially that picture, brought back
many memories for me. The team in the picture was
one of the best in the state. I recalled just why it was so
good. Yes, we had good pitchers, hitters, and fielders.
But what we did better than anyone was bunt. Our
coach believed in bunting. Every practice we had
bunting drills. Everyone on the team was good at
bunting.

Perhaps you are not a baseball fan and do not know about the fine art of bunting. Bunting is when a batter does not try to swing and get a hit. The batter, instead, turns or squares around, faces the pitcher, with hands apart on the bat, and attempts to tap the ball a few feet or yards in front of homeplate.

Why? Usually it is because there is a runner on first base and you want to move that runner to second base. This gets the runner in better scoring position. If someone comes up after you and gets a hit, a runner on second has a much better chance of scoring a run than a runner on first base.

Sometimes we would use the bunt in what was called a "squeeze play" when we had a runner on third base. When the pitcher throws the ball, the runner on third runs for home. Your job as batter is to bunt the ball, thus allowing the runner to score. If you miss the ball, the catcher catches the ball; and the runner is easily tagged out. You can see why players sometimes call this move "The Suicide." Our team had that play down to perfection.

True, bunting is not very exciting. A triple or homerun or grand slam is much more exciting. Bunting does not help your batting average either; for most of the time when you bunt, you get thrown out at first base. You see, another word for bunting is *sacrifice*. You sacrifice your chance for a news-making hit (or sometimes a strikeout) for the good of the team. You get thrown out at first base; but your teammate gets to second, that is, your team gets a better chance to win. Winning teams have good bunters, persons not afraid to sacrifice for the good of the team, even if it does not show up in the score book.

I do not know how, but the topic came up one day around the church. Our pastor and our coach were talking about something the church needed. I overheard the coach respond, "Pastor, sounds like what our church needs is more bunters."

That really puzzled me at the time. I could not see at all what bunting had to do with the church. But the pastor seemed to understand what our coach was saying. In fact, I later learned that the coach had volunteered to be a teacher in the youth Sunday school class.

Now I understand. "Winning" churches, like winning baseball teams, have good bunters, persons willing to sacrifice for the good of the team. The churches I know that are really growing and accomplishing things for God have lots of people who do not care who gets the credit for what is done. All they care about is bunting, doing what they can for the good of the team. Their names may not show up each Sunday in the bulletin, but they sit in quiet celebration; for they know that their efforts help make for a winning team.

I remember one game in a championship series. We were tied. We had a runner on first base, and it was my turn at bat. One out. The coach gave me the bunt signal. I really did not want to bunt. I thought I could get a hit off the pitcher. Besides, that would have gotten my name in the paper. But I did what I was told. I laid down a perfect bunt on the third base line. The runner on first advanced easily to second, but I was thrown out at first. I walked to the dugout a little down. But you know what? Our next batter hit a Texas leaguer right over the second baseman's head, and the runner on second scored the winning run. Nobody cheered louder than I did. Everybody put the runner and the boy who got the hit on their shoulders. But the coach came and put an arm around me.

Maybe what we do for Christ seems insignificant and goes largely unnoticed by many. But we know what we contribute and so does The Coach. Our bunting helps the team. That's all that matters.

Great Coach, you have given me and all your players many gifts and chosen us to be on your team. We are ready to play, even if you ask us to bunt. Put us in the game. Amen.

Fish Bones
and Bread Crumbs

[Jesus] said to them, "How many loaves have
you? Go and see." When they found out, they
said, "Five, and two fish." (Mark 6:38)

A SUNDAY SCHOOL TEACHER ASKED HER CLASS,
"What's your favorite Bible story?" One little boy said,
"I like the story where everyone loafs and fishes."

So do I. It's my favorite. (Wouldn't you know a story
about fish would be the favorite of someone named
Bass!) It must have been a favorite for the early Christians, too; for it is the only miracle story of Jesus
recorded in all four Gospels.

As far as the disciples were concerned, Jesus had
given them an impossible task—to feed five thousand
men (not counting women and children—and you
know how much they eat) with two fish and five small
barley loaves. But they had forgotten that Jesus had a
way of taking a little and making much from it.

My, can I identify with them! Most of us face tasks
and responsibilities that appear to be overwhelming.
The need seems so great and our resources so small.

I remember the first time I looked at the wrinkled little face of my newborn son. I felt two things—tremendous joy and terror. I knew that this little one would need so much from me. I checked my closet marked "Parental Supplies," and all I found was one dried up fish and a stale loaf of bread. But then I thought of this story; and it said to me, "That's enough. Just offer what you have, and I will feed the little one for you."

I have felt this same way as a teacher in the church. There are so many persons in the class with such varied needs. They come to sit at the table each week and look to me to provide some bread, something nourishing. Sometimes it is only a fish or two or the end pieces of a leftover loaf of bread. What I have to offer seems so meager in light of the hungry stomachs and souls I hear rumbling.

At no time, however, have I felt this more than in preaching. There have been times when I wish I had as much as a fish and piece of bread to offer. Sometimes I feel that I only have a fish bone and some crumbs. I remember one occasion on which I felt that I had not even offered that much. I wanted to go out the back door of the church rather than go to the front as people left.

On Monday morning, while I sat in my study, someone knocked at the door. It was a woman who had been a widow for years. I was not prepared for what she was about to tell me. She began by saying how much the sermon had meant to her. Well, I just about passed out and thought of requesting that she call the paramedics.

"You see," she said, "you spoke about how God does not want us to live in the past but to be open to the good gifts God wants to give us now. Well, you don't know this; but Wilbur [he was a widower in our community] asked me to marry him several weeks ago. Until yesterday, I had been telling him no, even though I do love him. I thought that if I remarried, I would be dishonoring my former husband and our children. But I've talked with my children, and they don't want me to live in the past anymore. So, I've accepted Wilbur's proposal; and we want you to marry us."

God took my one little fish bone and that morsel of bread and fed her. It was a miracle! To me, it was as great a miracle as that day by the Sea of Galilee.

We do not have to be adequate for every need or task that arises—as if we could be. Jesus does not ask us to give what we do not have. He asks only that we check our resources, offer him what we do have, and trust him to make much out of our little. When we do, miracles happen. People are fed.

Lord, you have called us to great tasks and our resources seem so meager. Help us to offer them anyway, trusting that even our little can be much in your hands. Amen.

Messenger in the Mall

Does not wisdom call,
   and does not understanding raise
      her voice?
On the heights, beside the way,
   at the crossroads she takes
      her stand;
beside the gates in front of the
      town;
   at the entrance of the portals
      she cries out.
(Proverbs 8:1-3)

I SAW HIM IN THE MALL. HE WAS ABOUT 5'6" AND WEARING a dark uniform that made you think of the air force or at least some branch of the military service. The cap was the kind you would see a policeman wearing . . . at least they used to wear them . . . short brim and looking like it was made of cardboard. On the collar of his coat on both sides was a large *S* in a circle of silver thread. He was holding a red metal bank that had a handle, and he was constantly rattling the change in it. Behind him were three angel trees covered with little paper angels that had the names and needs of little children throughout Roanoke, Virginia. Around the trees were brightly wrapped packages of all shapes and sizes, and people were dropping off more of them as I sat and watched.

There was something else about this jolly fellow standing there. I did not notice it at first. He only used one hand. His other hand was withered looking, drawn back toward his elbow. It was apparently quite unusable.

I walked up to him, put in a donation, and we started to talk. His name is Phillip Priest. He was thirty-six years old and had worked with the Salvation Army since he was fourteen. He was taking classes to become an officer (ordained) and his girlfriend was too. I asked him how the donations were going.

"Not as much as last year," he said. "People are kind of stingy this year for some reason."

I stood there looking at the people passing by, most holding armloads of presents to take to loved ones. It was obvious there was no shortage of money.

I got up the courage to ask about his hand.

He told me that it happened at birth . . . that the midwife "yanked" on his arm in such a way that permanent damage was caused. He was not bitter at all. It did not seem to bother him or hinder him in the least.

We talked about his plans, why he was doing what he was doing . . . and it all came around to the fact that he just loved Jesus and people . . . that he had no choice but to follow the path before him.

I thanked him for what he was doing and said that I would keep him in my prayers.

In the midst of the mall, among thousands of people out looking for gifts for themselves or those they love, stood a small man who spent day and night there seeking gifts not for himself but for others—little children, the hungry, the homeless. It was to me as if Jesus was standing there that day.

Lord, thank you for Phillip Priest and all those like him. They challenge and humble me in their unselfish giving and in their priorities. They are surely closer to the Kingdom than I often am. Bless him in his studies and in his marriage. Thank you for his witness in the midst of the mall. Amen.

Lend an Ear

You must understand this, my beloved: let everyone be quick to listen. (James 1:19)

I LOVE TO LISTEN TO NATIONAL PUBLIC RADIO'S *ALL Things Considered*. It is like a classic book or a cup of Earl Grey tea, something to be savored.

Recently they interviewed a scientist who has been studying the sounds or communication of elephants. She has made some fascinating discoveries. One is that elephants emit a sound too low for human ears to pick up. However, with her equipment, she can record the sound of the elephants and then play it at a faster speed so that we can hear it. Interesting that all that talking is going on, and we never hear it. Makes me wonder how many of the friends and strangers and family in our herds are trying to communicate the moans of their souls but no one hears.

The scientist noted that as she watched the elephants, quite often they would stop eating and stand still, their large ears standing out from the side of their heads like satellite dishes, listening to sounds, some of distress, coming from miles away. She called it "communal listening."

I know there are times to speak as individuals and as the church. But it seems to me that often what the world needs from us first is our ears and hearts attuned, opened, and engaged in communal listening, that we might hear the distress and pain from the human herd. Talkers, people with advice you can always find. But listeners? A whole community of ears?

I would hope this for each family and for the whole church, that we would be communal listeners. Please let us share with one another. Do not be afraid to share even your moans too deep for words. We will hear, for we will be listening. Friends and countrymen, lend them your ears!

Lord, you gave me two ears and only one mouth. Are you trying to tell me something? Amen.

Little Trees

But Moses' hands grew weary; so . . . Aaron and
Hur held up his hands, one on one side, and the
other on the other side; . . . so his hands were
steady.
(Exodus 17:12, RSV)

*T*HE AREA BETWEEN OUR SANCTUARY AND EDUCATIONAL
building was, well, ugly. It was mostly mud. This did
not bother the children in our church. They saw it as a
wonderful playground. Their parents did not exactly
see it that way. Tired of this eyesore, a committee was
appointed to come up with ideas for improvement.
Soon that area had grass growing, flower beds, some
benches, and a fountain. And to top it off several small
trees were planted.

One summer day a storm arose, pounding the
ground with rain and rattling my office windows in the
church. I happened to look out the window at those little trees that were then about five feet tall. The wind
was whipping them back and forth until they were left
almost touching the ground.

Our committee had an emergency meeting of sorts
and decided to place some steel rods beside each tree.
We then tied each tree to the rod beside it. A few days

later we had another storm. I looked out the window as the rain poured down and the wind blew. Each little tree was standing tall.

That same day I went to visit an elderly woman in the hospital. As I walked into the hospital room, I saw two church members, a man and his wife, standing beside her bed; one on each side. They were tenderly caring for her. I had seen them stand beside her in so many ways, even though she was not related to them in any way other than a sister in Christ. They visited her, took her to the doctor, to the grocery store, and even on vacation with them. They stood beside her like those steel rods beside the little storm-swept trees. Every time I visited her, she had to tell me of her love for them and how much they meant to her. They were steel rods for her, Aarons and Hurs, lifting her up.

When I got back to church, I walked out to look at the little trees with the steel rods. Suddenly it came to me that I am a lot like them. So many times in my life storms have threatened to blow me down. More than once I have found myself bent over by some unforeseen problem or trial, only to be gently lifted up and strengthened by strong Christian friends. So I stood there and said a prayer for the Aarons and Hurs God has sent to my side—friends, pastors, Sunday school teachers, coaches, family, and so many others.

As if in answer to that prayer, another thought came to me that day. Yes, others had held me up during storms; but how many little trees was I standing beside? From that day I have made it my business to be on the lookout for little trees who need someone to help them stand tall in the storms.

Lord, often we feel like small trees in a storm. Help us remember that we never face the storms alone. You are with us. You surround us and hold us up, often through strong and caring friends. Help us to be such friends to your other little trees. Amen.

The Stream

Wash me thoroughly from my iniquity,
and cleanse me from my sin.
(Psalm 51:2)

W HERE WE LIVE IN HOT SPRINGS, VIRGINIA, IS A RESORT called "The Homestead." It has wondrous mountain trails winding through the George Washington National Forest. I often find myself on one of those trails. The trail winds past lush trees in the spring and summer, which are decorated in the fall with every color under the sun. The many valleys and ravines seem to go on forever, and many have the most unusual rock formations (some look like ancient gray dinosaurs). I especially like seeing the variety of wildlife—chipmunks, squirrels, foxes, bobcats, deer, turkey, birds of all kinds, and even an occasional bear track (which is all I really wish to see in regard to bears).

I always see something on the trails that strikes a chord of joy or wonder in my soul. But nothing speaks to me more than a small stream that tumbles its way down from a mountain spring all the way to The Homestead. Even before I reach it, I can hear it singing to me in the distance. Many times I have seen deer and other forest creatures drawn to its singing and lapping up its song. My family has had many picnics there. We even take our dog, Shep; and he seems to love it more than any of us. The water is always cold. Just upstream I discovered that someone long ago built a crude springhouse over the stream. This little stream has been a favorite of humans and animals for a long time. I often wonder if Native Americans once camped by it and drank from its waters.

One day I stepped across the stream and dislodged several large stones that came crashing down into it, muddying its crystal clear water. I found myself feeling sad that I had so disturbed its beauty. But then, as I stood there and watched, something wondrous happened. Fresh, clean water continued flowing down from somewhere up the mountain, washing the muddy water away until it was clear again.

I realized as I watched that my life was often like that stream. I can really muddy up things sometimes. In fact, that very day I had been feeling soiled concerning some things in my life that I knew needed cleansing. If God can cleanse a muddy mountain stream, then surely God can cleanse me. So I found myself kneeling by the stream, praying a prayer of confession, and seeking forgiveness. Those simple actions opened the cleansing waters of God's grace that flowed into my soul. I felt clean.

When I got home, my daughter, then about three years old, had been playing in the yard. Most of our yard is covered with grass, but she had managed to find the few patches of dirt there. She was covered with dirt from head to toe. I took her inside and ran a bath for her. There was so much soil in the bathtub that we could have planted a large garden. When I took her out, wrapping a large, warm, white towel about her, she said, "Daddy, thanks for the bath. I feel so clean." And I said, "I know what you mean, honey. I know exactly what you mean."

God, like a loving parent, you bathe us in the baptismal tub, picking us up and wiping us off. We feel so clean! Help us remember our baptism when life soils us. Amen.

The Water Stick

Cast all your anxiety upon him, because he cares for you. (1 Peter 5:7)

S OME OF MY FONDEST MEMORIES OF MY CHILDHOOD are of the times I went to stay with my Grandfather Mitchell. (We called him "Papa.") He was about 5'11" with sparkling blue eyes. Papa was almost totally bald, which did not seem to bother him at all. In fact, he had a sign on his wall that said, "God only made a few perfect heads. The rest he covered with hair." He always wore a pair of blue overalls that were only fastened over one shoulder, the other strap dangling on his chest.

I loved Papa because he always had time for me. He had a potbellied stove in the center of his living room. By it sat a black stool with a square top on which rested a worn checkerboard. Papa taught me how to play checkers, all the while telling me stories about my father and long-deceased relatives.

Papa's house did not have indoor plumbing, something I thought was kind of cool at the time. There was a spring a good distance from his house. Papa had made for his shoulders a pole with a notch on each end in which to rest the handle of a bucket. Many times I walked with him across the field and into a green thicket, animal tracks all around it, and saw him fill buckets and carry them to the house.

One day I begged him to let me go and get the water alone. He finally gave in; and I ran down to the spring, carrying the buckets and pole. I filled both buckets to the top, placed them in just the right place, hooked the handles onto the pole, bent down and slipped the pole onto my shoulders, and then tried to stand. It was all I could do just to get the buckets a few inches off the ground. I stumbled forward, sloshing some of the water onto the dry summer ground. I struggled for a long time, finally looking up to see that I had made hardly any progress at all. My shoulders were aching, sweat was pouring into my eyes. Just when I thought I would have to give up, a cool shadow fell over me; and I looked up into the face of Papa.

"Need a hand?" he asked.

I shook my head no, my pride hurting just a bit. But all I managed to do was fall on my knees. "I think I can use that hand now," I muttered, realizing that the loss of a little pride was not so bad compared to breaking my shoulders. My grandfather reached down and took the pole off my shoulders as if it weighed nothing and then placed it on his broad shoulders. I remember how wonderful it felt to get rid of those heavy buckets. I felt like I was walking on air. I knew I could not have carried them much longer. I followed Papa to the house, he whistling some tune I had never heard.

Since then I have often looked at my own shoulders for the buckets I am still carrying there full of all the things I have put in them over the last year—guilt, sin, an unforgiving spirit, grudges, pains of the past I can do nothing about. I have to remember to allow Christ to take them onto his strong, broad shoulders. For he came and carried a large pole, a cross upon his back, for us because we could not carry it. How foolish to keep trying.

Just a footnote: I finally managed to convince Papa to get indoor plumbing. But I still have that old pole with the bucket notches. It is resting in the corner of my study. Right beside it on the desk is a wooden cross. I try each day to look at them and to give up something so that I will have the strength to take on something else that day for the One who cares and carries so much for me.

Lord, help me to be honest with you and myself this day. Help me to name at least one thing I have been carrying around for too long. Then give me the humility and wisdom to hand it over to you, for I know you care for me. Amen.

Closed Doors

They went through the region of Phrygia and
Galatia, having been forbidden by the Holy
Spirit to speak the word in Asia. (Acts 16:6)

*H*OW I ENVIED PEOPLE, EVEN IN ELEMENTARY
school, who seemed to know exactly what they wanted
to be when they grew up. Some already had their life all
planned out and arranged. They knew what college
they would attend, what major they would choose, and
even where they wanted to live and work.

It has not been that way for me. For a long time in
my life it seemed, vocation wise, that I was running
into one closed door after another. I thought I was
going in the way God wanted, only to discover the path
was blocked. So I backed off and headed in another
direction until I finally came to a door, pastoral min-
istry, that swung open wide for me. I have to admit that
for much too long I would stand and try to knock down
those closed doors rather than moving along to new
ones.

My brother had much the same experience. He
changed majors about six times in college. He often

confided in me that this bouncing off of closed doors was leaving him bruised, sore, angry, and frustrated. What did God want him to do with his life? Where did God want him to go? There had to be a door open somewhere. Come to find out it was close to home. He took over the cabinet and carpentry shop from our father and has proven to be quite good at his craft. A door was finally opened.

When Paul and his companions tried to enter Asia on their second missionary journey, they ran into a closed door. We are not told the precise obstacle to their work there, only that they saw it as divine guidance.

Next they tried to enter Bithynia, "but the Spirit of Jesus did not allow them." They ran right into another closed door. Yet they were still convinced that God was guiding them. Later, Paul had a vision of a man from Macedonia. He pleaded with Paul to come and help them. So he went and met with great success (Acts 16:7-34).

Sometimes God guides us like Paul. Yet we cannot always wait for absolute assurance as to the precise will of God before we act. Often we must step out in faith, acting on what we believe to be God's will and trusting God to guide us. When we do this, God may then guide us by closing doors. Blocked paths, frustrated plans, and wrong decisions will not discourage us, however, if, like Paul, we see them as ways God can guide us to fruitful service elsewhere.

God, so often we have run into closed doors and stood there for the longest time pounding on them. Give us wisdom to know when you have closed a door and faith to keep on walking until we find the one you have opened for us. Amen.

Clouds

How clearly the sky reveals
 God's glory!
How plainly it shows what he
 has done! . . .
No speech or words are used,
 no sound is heard;
yet their message goes out to all
 the world
 and is heard to the ends of the
 earth.
   (Psalm 19:1, 3, TEV)

I HAVE ALWAYS LOVED CLOUDS. I LIKE TO SIT OUT IN THE yard and watch them as they come across the mountains. God displays a grand show on this giant sky screen.

It seems to me that the clouds the last few weeks have been especially gorgeous. One day a line of grayish-white clouds crested the mountain range for as far as the eye could see. Another day, while driving to town, I saw that gray storm clouds in the distance had shimmering shafts of sunlight streaming down through them. No special effects artist in Hollywood could ever hope to match the sight. My wife had to tell me to keep my eyes on the road.

I have always loved clouds. . . .

Did you know that clouds play an important role in the Bible?

God sets the rainbow in the clouds . . . a promise of God's presence and protection.

Read Exodus and see how many times God's glory appears to Moses from a cloud (Exodus 16:10). And a pillar of clouds led the children of Israel through the wilderness during the day (Psalm 78:14).

The psalmist describes God's love as so great that it extends to the clouds:

Your steadfast love, O LORD,
    extends to the heavens,
your faithfulness to the clouds. (Psalm 36:5)

God speaks to Jesus and the three disciples out of a cloud on the mount of Transfiguration (Matthew 17:1-8).

Jesus says that the Son of Man will come again in the clouds (Mark 14:62).

I was driving on Interstate 64 from Lexington, Virginia, to Covington recently. The mountains are breathtaking there. Suddenly, ahead of me, appearing just over the mountain range were some clouds set ablaze by the sun. What astounded me was that one cloud was horizontal and the other vertical, and they crossed each other. Why is it that I never have a camera with me when I need one? For there, lifted up in the sky, was the glory of God revealed to me that day in the shape of a cross made of clouds. I could not help but think about another cross on another cloudy day long ago lifted to the sky. It was not made of clouds but of wood. It was not holding air and moisture but holding the very love of God.

As I watched this cloud cross, I had the strange feeling that it had circled the world in just that same shape . . . its message truly going out to all the world. For me, it was just one other way God was trying to show me, to show us all that we are loved . . . loved so much that God's own Son died for us.

Strange, too, was the fact that this cross made of clouds went before me all the way home. I found myself singing the verse to a chorus I learned as a child: "The world behind me, the cross before . . . no turning back, no turning back."

Lord, we are your clouds, too, we who have decided to follow Jesus. May we be as faithful in lifting him up, in letting his glory and love show forth in us, as the clouds that even now are drifting above us. Amen.

Cross

I pray that you may have the power to comprehend, with all the saints, what is the breadth and length and height and depth, and to know the love of Christ that surpasses all knowledge, so that you may be filled with the fullness of God. (Ephesians 3:18-19)

I HAVE A FRIEND WHO USES WORDS AND PHRASES FROM the Lord's Prayer to help him in prayer and meditation. He says, "Our Father. . . ." Then he writes the words on paper and places the paper where he will see it often that week. He lets those words sink into his thoughts and bring to him whatever images and truths they will.

I have tried his method but find that I often need an object or some image to assist me in praying and meditating. For me, the primary object has been the cross.

A large cross hangs in our sanctuary. It is not made of polished wood or shining metal. In fact, it is crude, covered with splinters, and weather-worn. I imagine the original cross would not have been much different. This cross is suspended from the ceiling of the sanctuary right in the middle, so that wherever you are, you can see it.

I have started a custom of entering the sanctuary on Sundays and any day by pausing for a moment to gaze at the cross. It helps focus my mind and prepare my heart for worship as I contemplate what God has done for us all in Christ.

A friend made me a small oak cross that sits on a wooden stand. I have it on my desk. It is the first thing I see each morning when I enter the office, and it does much the same thing for me as does the large one in our sanctuary.

One day as my eyes came to rest on this cross, I began to see it in a whole new way.

I noticed that it points down. That tells me that no matter how low we sink, how far we stray from God, God's love in Christ can reach down to us. The love of God in Christ is such that the Apostles' Creed says, "He descended into hell." The love of God even reaches down to those in hell! Then surely God's love can reach us.

Then I looked at the cross beam of the cross and saw that it points outward. The love of Christ extends to all. It is inclusive, not exclusive. "For God so loved the world. . . ." It was no mere accident that the arms of Christ were stretched out on the cross. For on the cross, Jesus looked out over the whole world, to every nation and every generation; and he spread wide his arms to embrace us all.

Finally, I realized that the cross points up. That tells me that the love of God in Christ continues to love us all the way to heaven. This love gives us eternal life.

The first funeral service I had was at the graveside. As I spoke the words, "Dust to dust, ashes to ashes," the funeral director poured sand onto the coffin. He did not just pour it in any fashion. He made one long strand and then a strand across it. He made a cross. How appropriate, I thought. The cross, a symbol of death, is now in Christ the greatest symbol of love—a love that not even death can destroy. Nothing, not even death, can take us away from the love of God that is ours through Christ Jesus.

God, bring before our eyes each day the cross of Christ so that throughout the day, whether we look down, around, or up, we might be reminded that there is no place any of us can ever be that your love cannot reach and hold us. Amen.

"I See Him!"

And [Jesus] was transfigured before them, and
his clothes became dazzling white, such as no
one on earth could bleach them. (Mark 9:2-3)

N OT LONG AGO I WAS WALKING IN A SHOPPING
mall in Charlottesville, Virginia, when I noticed a
group of people staring at something in a display window. Curious, I walked over to see what was happening. They were staring at a strange poster sitting on an
easel. The poster was brightly colored and had what
seemed to be meaningless symbols and patterns.

"Must be new age art," someone mumbled behind
me. "Never did understand that stuff."

Suddenly, a person in the crowd said, "I see him! I
see him!" pointing at the poster.

"See what? See who?" everyone asked together.

"Well, I'm not sure who it is; and I don't want to spoil
it for you," she said.

I thought to myself, "Yeah, right. You don't see anything."

But then another person said, "I see him too!"

We all looked at the poster with greater concentra-
tion. But after a few minutes, many walked away, shak-
ing their heads.

"Can you tell me what's going on?" I asked one of the persons who said she had seen him.

"This is a hologram or 3-D picture," she explained. "If you look at it in just the right light and at just the right angle, you will see an image hidden there."

"Really?" I replied, still doubtful.

"Well, it's not easy. It takes time. But there he is. Don't you see him?" she said.

I stared until my head ached. "I don't see anything," I replied, adding, "There's not a *Candid Camera* crew set up around here, is there?"

She smiled and said, "Don't give up." Then she walked away before I could ask for some aspirin.

I must have looked at that poster a dozen times that night with the same result. On the way out of the mall, I decided to give it one last try. As I looked at the poster, bending my head to the side, the symbols started to fade and a face began to form. "I see him! I see him!" I said right out loud, grinning at the complete strangers behind me. Then I realized whose face it was I was seeing for the first time—Jesus. And there were three crosses in the background.

I spent an hour after that trying to convince and help others see the face there. It was fun watching their faces light up when they saw him too.

Loving God, help us in some new way each day to be able to say, "I see him!" and to be able to help others see him too. Amen.

Shadows on the Sand

> . . . so that they would search for God and per-
> haps grope for God and find God—though
> indeed God is not far from each one of us. For
> in God we live and move and have our being.
> (Acts 17:27-28, author's paraphrase of NRSV)

*I*T WAS THE SUMMER OF 1995. WE WERE ON VACATION AT Virginia Beach. I invited my daughter, Meredith, to go for a walk on the beach after sunset. The waves were crashing into the beach, sending a fine ocean mist into the early night sky that made me feel like I was walking in a dream world. The sounds of surf and wind seemed muffled by a deep quietness, a kind of solitude in which the beach reveled after a day of being trampled upon by so many feet. The footprints had been washed away, all except ours, which the surf began to fill and erase behind us.

Meredith never walks anywhere. Walking for her is like jogging for me. When she is not running, she is doing flips, cartwheels, and somersaults. I hardly ever see her blond hair resting on her tiny shoulders, for it streams behind her because of her perpetual motion. So, needless to say, she was some distance ahead of me.

I saw Meredith stop and then sit down on a ridge of sand carved out by the ceaseless pounding of the surf. She rested her elbows on her knees and looked out at the ocean. Little did I know as I walked up to her that I was about to be transformed by one of those mystical moments.

I approached Meredith slowly, thinking it a little unusual to see her so still and quiet. I was tempted to speak to her, but words did not seem appropriate. I was enjoying this all too rare moment with her in a place far from all the pastoral duties that weighed so heavily upon me.

As I stood there in front of Meredith, I noticed three spotlights on top of the condo behind us—one on each end and one in the middle—all shining down toward the beach. Then she stood up and there appeared before me three shadows on the sand . . . her shadows . . . all similar yet with subtle differences. One person . . . three shadows.

Time seemed to stand still for that moment. I could barely hear the waves or feel the wind. As I stood there in those three shadows on the sand, I felt immersed in a profound sense of being in the presence of the Father, the Son, and the Holy Spirit—the Holy Trinity, the Three-in-One.

As Meredith stood up and started down the beach again, I walked (jogged) beside her; and those three shadows stayed with us down the beach. Needless to say, I will never look at shadows in the same way again.

Lord, you have taught me to always be on the lookout for you, even in shadows that may cross my path. I know that you are as close to me as my own shadow. Help me be more alert to the countless ways you will come to me this day. Amen.

Dancing in the Shadows

Yea, though I walk through the valley of the shadow of death, I will fear no evil: for thou art with me; thy rod and thy staff they comfort me. (Psalm 23:4, KJV)

*M*Y FATHER TOOK ME ON OUR FIRST CAMPING TRIP together when I was eight years old. We set up camp and then went on a hike down a forest trail. Before we could get back to camp it got dark. The moon was rising; and a breeze blew through the forest, casting eerie shadows around us as we walked. I took hold of my father's hand and squeezed it tightly. The shadows seemed to be giant monsters with large arms reaching out to grab me. I looked up at him and whispered, "Daddy, I don't like the shadows. They scare me."

My father knelt down, sitting me on one of his knees. He stretched out one of his hands into a shadow at our feet. The shadow looked like a hungry mouth. He turned his hand over in the shadow and then slowly pulled it back. Then he said, "Put your hand on mine." I reluctantly rested my hand on his. He then slowly put our hands into the shadow and said, "See? Don't be afraid of the shadows. They can't hurt you."

To be sure shadows can be scary. David knew this well. He spent much of his early life as a shepherd. Often he would have to lead the sheep through rocky clefts and valleys where there were lots of shadows and the sheep were fearful. I'm told it does not take all that much to scare sheep, anyway. But David knew, as their shepherd, that no shadow could harm his sheep.

When David wrote Psalm 23, he recognized God as his shepherd. He knew that God would lead him through the shadowy valleys, just as he had led his own sheep. God could even lead David safely through the valley of the shadow of death.

But let me tell you the rest of the story of our first camping trip.

After I put my hand in the shadow, I slowly put in one foot . . . then the other . . . until I was standing completely in the shadow. I smiled up at my father and began to dance right there in the shadow. I danced through the shadows all the way to camp, glancing up now and then to make sure my father was still there. When we got back, my father made a glorious camp-fire; and from its light we made funny shadow creatures on the side of the tent.

Shadows can startle us, make us run into true danger that will hurt us. But in and of themselves, they are powerless. They cannot harm us. In fact, shadows are only reminders that light is present; for they cannot exist without light. So, do not fear the shadows. Think of The Light above them. Remember that the Shepherd is with you even in the shadows. So dance in them until you reach camp.

God of light and shadows, we love the sunny meadows and bright, cloudless days. But we fear the dark valleys full of shadows and unknown things; and we wonder why we must walk through them. Help us remember that we are not alone—that you walk there with us and that you lead us through them, never abandoning us there. Lead us, Good Shepherd, to the light of your camp, to the warmth of your presence; and we will laugh together at the shadows. Amen.

Fortress

In you, O Lord, I take refuge;
  let me never be put to shame. . . .
Be to me a rock of refuge,
  a strong fortress, to save me,
  for you are my rock and my fortress.
  (Psalm 71:1, 3)

I FOUND A CARDBOARD BOX IN OUR CLOSET RECENTLY. I took it down and looked inside. There I found hundreds of photographs we had taken over the years—from our honeymoon, to the births of Michael and Meredith, to various significant events in their lives, to photo memories of the many trips we have taken together. Then, in a small package, I found several photos of a trip we took to Fort Macon on the coast of North Carolina when Meredith was still in a stroller and Michael was about four. Among them were photos of the family standing beside the massive walls of the old fort.

The memories of that day came flooding back into my mind . . . of a cavernous stone room with a ceiling darkened by campfires from long ago. We retreated there when one of the many summer thunderstorms decided to pay us a visit that day. We stood in that stone fortress while the lightning flashed, the thunder shook the ground, and torrents of rain fell and drained quickly toward the ocean.

After an especially loud clap of thunder, Michael gripped my leg and looked around with eyes wide with fear. "Daddy, I'm scared," he whispered. I knelt and pointed to the massive stone walls that surrounded us. "See those?" I asked. He nodded. "They are several feet thick all around us. We are perfectly safe here. Nothing can hurt us," I reassured him. My words seemed to calm him, especially, I suppose, because I was so calm myself.

Together we experienced a profound sense of peace and security behind those walls. I thought of the soldiers who had long ago also taken cover behind those walls as the great storm of the Civil War raged around them. I wondered if they felt as safe there as I did that day.

I cannot help but think of this experience also when I read the psalmist talking about God being his rock fortress, his hiding place, his refuge. The psalmist does this many times in Psalm 27.

The LORD is my light and my salvation;
    whom shall I fear?
The LORD is the stronghold of my life;
    of whom shall I be afraid?
When evildoers assail me . . .
Though an army encamp against me, . . .
    yet I will be confident. . . .
For he will hide me in his shelter
    in the day of trouble;

he will conceal me under the cover of his tent;
    he will set me high on a rock. . . .
                (selected verses from Psalm 27)

And in one of my favorites, Psalm 46:1, he sings:

God is our refuge and strength,
    a very present help in trouble.

The psalmist used the most secure image he could find to try to express the confidence he had in God and in God's protective care that he had experienced from the day of his birth. God was a mighty rock fortress surrounding his life, giving him profound peace and security when enemies threatened from without and fears from within. This mighty fortress was always there for him, open and ready for him to retreat to and rest whenever he needed it. It was not really a fortress made of stone blocks but of blocks hewn by his faith and trust, by every memory he had of how God had been with him all his life. He is absolutely confident now, as he is an old man with failing health and perhaps fear of death, that God still surrounds him like a mighty fortress.

How we tried to teach our dog, Shep, to seek shelter in the doghouse we bought for him when the snow and sleet began to fall. He would go into it for a little while, but then he would come back out.

How foolish to stay out in the cold and storm when shelter is right there. How foolish it would have been that day at Fort Macon to stay out in the thunder and lightning when such a protective shelter was right there beside us.

God, the storms rage outside us and inside us. The storms make us feel sometimes that we are all alone, afraid, powerless, and without shelter; for they rage so. But we know we are never without shelter. We are never alone. We are never powerless. You, O God— your Son, your Spirit, your Word—are mighty walls around us. Truly, within such a fortress, of what or whom shall we be afraid? Amen.

Amish Tables

When the hour came, he took his place at the
table, and the apostles with him. (Luke 22:14)

ONE SUMMER WE WENT TO AMISH COUNTRY IN
Lancaster County, Pennsylvania. We toured a model of
an Amish homestead built very much like Amish
homes today. Amish woodcrafters had made all the fur-
niture. So much there stood out to me but nothing
more so than the table in the kitchen—a simple, hand-
made table, perhaps of oak. It looked used, scarred by
the plates, pots, and pans of many meals laid out on it.
But, like everything else in that house, it was very prac-
tical; for the guide told us that it was made in such a
way as to be easily expanded for new additions to the
family.

The thought came to me that the Lord's Table must
also be an Amish table. It is made to expand and has
expanded over the centuries to make room for new
additions to the family. This table extends around the
world!

I remember growing up as the oldest of five children. With all our friends and relatives, we had company all the time—usually at dinnertime. Ever notice how some relatives and neighbors have this down to an art—arriving just as you sit down to eat?

My father was a carpenter. He made a long picnic-like kitchen table from heart pine. There were long benches on the sides and ends, for we needed lots of room. Anyway, when friends and relatives arrived, he would wave them to the table and say, "Always room for one more." And they became a member of the family through sharing that meal.

Some feel excluded from the table. They hunger for love, acceptance, and fellowship. The good news is that the Lord's Table is a long table and that the Host of this sacred meal waves everyone over, saying, "Always room for one more."

Loving Host, how hungry we are! Spread out on your table we see and smell the most delicious food. Thank you for saving a place for each of us. Amen.

The Jelly Jars

This is my body that is for you. Do this in
remembrance of me. . . . This cup is the new
covenant in my blood. Do this, as often as you
drink it, in remembrance of me.
(1 Corinthians 11:24, 25)

I TOOK THE OLD MASON JAR FROM THE
refrigerator. I was about to unscrew the shiny brass lid
when I noticed, written in blue marker, the following:
BB Jelly '95 BHR. I knew immediately what it meant:
Blue Berry Jelly, Made in 1995, by Bennie Harold Rackley (my father-in-law, who died suddenly in 1996 of a
heart attack while standing at the kitchen sink making
some other delicious item for his family).

The sweetest sorrow came over me as I held that jar.
I started having images of this kind, godly man out
planting those blueberry bushes in his backyard (which
I had seen and eaten from many times); watering and
fertilizing them; covering them with plastic in the winter; protecting them from pests (though I was one pest
he could not get rid of); watching them daily for signs
of fruit; then picking those berries, preparing them,
putting them in jars . . . putting so much of himself in
this simple gift. The wonderful, strange feeling came

over me that he was in that jar . . . that I was communing with him still.

The jelly has always been good, but it has had a deeper sweetness since then. When I share this jelly with my family around the table, it seems as if Harold is there, present with us. I want to put an extra chair at the table.

As I dipped some of the jelly onto a piece of homemade bread and sipped from a cup of juice that morning, Holy Communion suddenly took on a new meaning for me. When you take up the bread and cup, look for the writing: BB, A.D. 31, JC—Body and Blood of Jesus Christ, broken and shed for us long ago. How very much of himself, his life's blood, he put into the elements. Simple items were infused with new meaning, new sweetness. For if those we love can come to us in jars of jelly, how much more can the Risen Christ come and be present with us and in us through the cup and the bread? So, when we gather around the table for Communion, let's pull up an extra chair; for Christ is here.

Loving God, everywhere we look we see things that others have given us and in them given us something of themselves. When we see these things, we remember these persons; and it is almost as if they are present with us again. As we partake of the cup and bread, may the Christ come and be our honored guest—not just at our table but in our hearts. Amen.

The Bird Feeder

Consider the birds of the air; they neither sow nor reap nor gather into barns, and yet your heavenly Father feeds them. Are you not of more value than they? (Matthew 6:26, author's paraphrase of NRSV)

I am the bread of life. Whoever comes to me will never be hungry, and whoever believes in me will never be thirsty. (John 6:35)

I STOOD LOOKING OUT THE WINDOW IN AWE AS THEY came . . . from all directions . . . all sizes, all colors under the heavens . . . flocking together at the bird feeder my wife had just placed in the tree in our yard.

Blue jays, sparrows, cardinals, black birds, tiny ones with a spot of yellow on their wings, doves, and woodpeckers . . . they kept coming . . . making room for more . . . even for gray squirrels and chipmunks, for they all were hungry. . . .

They kept leaving and returning, for there was plenty for all and room for all that came. When they returned, it was as if they had told their families and friends where to come for food and escorted them there.

I noticed that some of the birds actually landed on the feeder and began vigorously raking out seeds that fell all over the ground for their friends waiting below.

Then, together, they began to chirp and sing, not in anger or frenzied selfish feeding, but joyous music to my ears. It was a celebration, a festival, a feast of feathered friends.

As I watched, I had a vision of sorts . . . the birds changed into people from all countries . . . all colors, all sizes, men, women, children, the rich, the poor, the starving. . . .

The feeder transformed into a table that had on it delicious, sweet-smelling loaves of bread, surrounded by cups of wine filled to overflowing.

They kept coming, for there was a place for everyone.

The Host, smiling, said, "Come and dine, all of you, for there is food for all." And they did come, united by their hunger and the generosity of the Host . . . and they left, only to come back with those who were also hungry. And they began to sing. . . .

God of birds and beasts, of all creatures great and small, you provide well for your creation. What variety of provision! It is as though the whole world is your table that you set each day for all your creations. How you must love us all, that not even a little sparrow falls to the ground without you knowing and caring. As we sit at your table this and each day, help us to be truly thankful and to break forth with all your creatures in the joyous singing of your praises. Amen.

In My Father's Shoes

Quickly, bring out a robe—the best one—and put it on him; put a ring on his finger and sandals on his feet. (Father concerning the prodigal son in Luke 15:22)

I FOUND THEM WHILE RUMMAGING THROUGH MY closet looking for a suitcase. They are not expensive and would mean nothing special to anyone except me. They are made of tanned leather, fading brown, with rubber soles and dark brown strings. They would probably be overlooked in a yard sale. They were my father's shoes. Mom gave them to me soon after my father's death about five years ago. We wore about the same size.

I put them in the closet back then, for it was just too painful looking at them or even thinking about wearing them. I tried them on today. As I put on the second shoe, a strange warmth seemed to begin in my feet and to spread to the depth of my soul. It was as if my father was present with me again, his love and kindness filling me, his gentle laughing eyes looking at me.

Dad, I can wear your shoes but I can never fill them . . .

I wish I had told you more often how much you mean to me . . .

thanked you more for all those hard days spent with saw and hammer to provide for us . . .

for coming home, tired as you were, but still spending hours tossing a baseball with me in the yard . . .

for the many times you took me fishing and, though you named me Bass, not worrying too much that I was not much of a fisherman. . . .

for all the times you prayed for me . . .

for not sending me to church but taking me . . .

for teaching me and showing me the love of Christ . . .

for the countless things a father does and worries about that I did not know until I became a father. . . .

You leave big shoes to fill, Dad. . . .

But you wouldn't want me trying to fill your shoes, would you? I can hear you now, "Walk in your own shoes, Son."

I will, Dad. But thanks for your shoes, for your loving soul that even now warms me, encourages and challenges me. . . .

So, I'll keep these shoes. I'll wear them. God, help me to leave such shoes behind in the closets of my children, such a soul, such a legacy of love and sacrifice. Amen.

Lord, I give you thanks this day for my parents and all those who took such care to love and teach me. Truly you have loved and blessed me through them. But I pray this day also for those whose parents have not loved them, who have, in fact, abused them, and that pain still remains with them. May they somehow know in you, God, the loving Parent they may have never had. May they hear you welcome them home; and may they receive the robe, ring, and shoes you have for them in your house. Amen.

The Coat

Then the saying that is written will be fulfilled:
"Death has been swallowed up
in victory."
"Where, O death, is your victory?
Where, O death, is your sting?"
(1 Corinthians 15:54-55)

*Y*OU DID NOT KNOW BENNIE HAROLD RACKLEY. HE was my father-in-law. In the late summer of 1996, he was standing at his kitchen sink in Momeyer, North Carolina, when he had a massive heart attack and died.

I was home alone that day when the call came. I know many of you have been in the same situation. I sat in stunned silence. I could not believe it. But my first thoughts were not of myself but of my wife, Debbie. I was going to have to tell her.

My son, fifteen years old then, got home from school before Debbie. I told him. We sat in silence, waiting for her to come home. My heart just seemed to shatter inside me when I saw her at the front door, walking through with her usual bright, radiant smile. I had to tell her that her father . . . he felt like my father, too . . . was dead. The three of us stood there, holding one another, sobbing. I have had to tell others that their father, mother, brother, sister, or child has died; but nothing, nothing was ever so difficult for me as this.

The next couple of weeks are a blur. There was so much to do . . . we lived so far away . . . and the pain, the waves of grief just kept washing over us all . . . all we could do was hold on to one another.

Weeks later, when Debbie and her sisters were trying to clean up in the home in which they were reared, they came across many of Harold's clothes. They gave some of them to me, since we wore the same size. I have not been able to even look at them until recently while searching through the closets for items to donate to a church yard sale. Among them was a Sunday coat I had seen Harold wear many times. It is gray with light blue lines running up and across. Nothing fancy about it.

I took the coat off the hanger and looked it over. I was about to hang it back up when I noticed something in the inside pocket. It was a folded piece of paper . . . a church bulletin Harold had tucked there the last time he had worn the coat. The bulletin cover was light purple with a Bible open to Mark 15 and 16. Behind and beside the Bible were white lilies and one bright candle. Written in script at the top in dark purple was the word *Alleluia!* (which means "Praise the Lord!").

Do you know what worship service this bulletin was for?

Easter! Easter Sunday, April 7, 1996!

Of all that could have been in that pocket, of all the fifty-two Sundays in the year, the one and only item in

Harold's coat was the bulletin that proclaimed the message of Easter!

I had been feeling like it was Good Friday for so long, but now Easter started to come for me in this deeply personal way. So, my friends, in the midst of your Good Fridays, just remember, Easter is coming!

Alleluia!

Alleluia, indeed!!!

God of Easter, God of the living, we praise you that your love is such that nothing can take us away from you, not even death. Thank you for the little but profound reminders you give of this great truth in the midst of our sorrow and loss. Amen.

A Strange Place for Christmas Lights

The people who sat in darkness
have seen a great light,
and for those who sat in the region
and shadow of death
light has dawned.
(Matthew 4:16)

I COULD HARDLY BELIEVE MY EYES. I PULLED THE CAR over to the side of the road and got out to take a closer look. No. I wasn't seeing things. It was real.

It was the Advent season. To celebrate that season most of us put lights up inside our house and outside. But I had never seen lights here before.

You see, there is a graveyard in a field close to where my wife's parents lived. Some of their ancestors are buried there, and some of the graves predate the War Between the States. Many years ago someone planted evergreen trees around that graveyard. I remembered how lovely the trees were and the pleasantness of their fresh smell. They filled the air that night with that sweet scent of evergreen.

But that night, there was something new and wonderful about that place. Someone had put beautiful white lights all over those trees. That place of death was circled and illuminated by Christmas lights!

I remember saying out loud, "What a strange place for Christmas lights."

But the more I thought about it, the more it made sense to me. I think I understand what the person who put up those lights was trying to say. Christmas means that light has come into every part of this dark world, even into the darkness of death. Christmas changes everything! In the Christ Child light and life are given that darkness and death cannot take away.

Usually we think of this theme at Easter. But without Christmas, there would be no Easter. That is what the Christmas lights on the cemetery trees proclaimed to me.

"What a strange place for Christmas lights."

No. Not at all.

God of light, Christmas finds many of us sitting in the darkness; for the death of someone close has seemed to shut out all the light. The joy of this season seems to have fled from us. Our thoughts are constantly being drawn to a dark cemetery. Help us, God of light, to see even shining there the light of life that you give through your unspeakable gift at Christmas. Let there be light for us all who sit in darkness, even the darkness of death. Amen.

Blessings of the Bells

Weeping may endure for a night, but joy
cometh in the morning.
(Psalm 30:5, KJV)

*I*T WAS A WEEK MANY WILL NEVER FORGET. PRINCESS Diana had died. I found myself feeling profound grief. I was one of the millions around the world who watched as the coffin of the princess was taken into the cathedral. Then I heard it—one lone, sorrowful bell rang each minute, echoing through the streets and to the far corners of the world until the coffin disappeared inside the church. That bell expressed so well the depth of grief so many felt. How it proclaimed to our hearts the message that we all come to such solemn moments, to sorrow and death; for the bell must also toll for each of us.

But then, when the coffin was being taken out of the cathedral, that one bell was joined, so it seemed to me, by a heavenly host of bells pealing out notes of great joy. How the bells rang that day! They proclaimed that death was not the final word, for we go out of this life to the joyous resurrection bells ringing and singing out the good news of Easter. We may leave with the sound of a single bell tolling, but we arrive in the heavenly places to a symphony of bells.

So, with the sound of that lone bell a memory, replaced by the joyous chorus of its brothers and sisters, I go out to face the world, renewed, reassured, more determined than ever to serve the Great Bell Ringer, whose joyous music fills my heart.

Bless, Lord, my friends who are reading these words. Let them become bells this day and each day of their lives. May they always hear the bells, be blessed by their message, and fill the world with joy and hope. Best of all, may they continue to hear you in every bell, in every sound, and see you in every blade of rustling grass. Amen.